Faith Over Fear

*"Your dreams do not have an expiration date. So take
a deep breath and try again."*

Efe Fruci

Hi Jodi,

Thank you for attending
Smashing limiting beliefs
keep on smashing all
the negative.

You've a champion and I
am cheering and rooting
for you.

Love
Efe.

Publisher: Independent Publishing Network

Published date: July 12, 2019

ISBN: 978-1-78972-366-3

Printed and bound in the United Kingdom by Bounce Design Oxford, 101 Magdalen Road, Oxford, OX4 1RG

Distributed in the United Kingdom by ET Grace Enterprise LTD, 10 Beech Court, Wokingham Road, Hurst, Berkshire, United Kingdom, RG10 0RQ

For Information about custom editions, special sales, and premium and corporate purchase, please contact Fearless and Empowered at +447501279068 or sales@fearlessandempowered.org

Book design by Tom Fruci

Cover design by Efe Fruci

Cover and Layout editing by Bounce Design

Biography picture by Jessie Whealy Photography

I wrote this book as an amalgamation of my thoughts, experiences, and lessons learned in my personal and professional journey.

This series of positive affirmations I have used while struggling with low self-esteem, lack of self-confidence, health struggles, self-doubts, feeling like I wasn't enough in my past relationships and when my life fell apart. It also acts as a reminder of where I have come from, what I have been through, where I am and where I can go.

I have built myself up using these steps to take back control of my life, to turn my pain into my power, my struggles into my strengths and used it to face my fears and overcome so many difficult moments in my life.

Faith Over Fear helps you transition, commit to new routines and achieve a healthy work-life balance and to have more faith in yourself.

I hope it motivates you to live an unshakeable, unstoppable life of self-confidence, self-acceptance and self-compassion by seeing how I transformed all my negatives into a positive, achieved the unachievable all the while building a legacy for my family, building a future I desire and deserve and how you can do it too.

Be sure to repeat to yourself the self-declaration before you begin your journey.

Table of Contents

Self-Declaration

"I am whole just by being.

I realize I am enough when I showed myself that I need do nothing to deserve love.

I have nothing to prove to anyone and I do not need to impress others but myself.

I am good enough for me because I am smart, beautiful, honest, kind, a priceless being, unique and loved by me.

I am comfortable with the woman I am now, the woman I am growing and maturing to be.

And as long as I am blessed to live in this magnificent planet, I will continue to show kindness to myself as I am whole.

I am enough because I am and I know now that I have always been enough all this time"

Efe Fruci

Introduction

Inspired by my personal experiences, I am sharing the tools and techniques that I have developed along my journey. Included are some inspirational quotes that have motivated me throughout my life, aiding my personal growth, shaped my view of the world and how I see myself today.

My aim and vision is that this book brings light into your moments of darkness to show you that you are loved, valued, worthy and that you matter simply because you exist.

May this book bring you hope when you feel hopeless, motivate and encourage you to appreciate all aspects of your life through your own pains and struggles, help you celebrate all your wins in life and celebrate who you are. Who you are becoming as you grow into being the best version of yourself.

Now commit to yourself, grow and be challenged as you begin living your life of purpose.

This book is designed for you, so use the blank pages in each series to write answers to the questions asked and journal your thoughts, feelings, and emotions from each topic.

Series Overview

Series 1: My Life Has Purpose

Series 2: My Potential is Limitless

Series 3: I Am Fearless

Series 4: I Am Confident

Series 5: I Have Value and Worth

Series 6: I Am Enough. I Am Loved

Series 7: I Have The Power Of Choice

Series 8: I Have A Future

Series 9: I Know MY Identity

Series 10: I Can. I Will

Goals

Before you begin this book, set out a goal in mind of what you want to achieve on your journey to creating a life of excellence. Write it down in the space below as a daily reminder.

Objectives

- **Build** your self-confidence, self-esteem and personal development.
- **Find** your identity and your life's calling.
- **Identify** your personal strengths and your motivations to pursue your dreams.
- **Empower** yourself to understand that you are capable of positively transforming your life and influencing the people in and around your world.
- **Motivate**, equip and empower you to set and achieve your personal goals.
- **Encourage** you to know that you can turn your struggles and challenges into your strengths and opportunities.

Gratitude

Gratitude:

The quality of being thankful; readiness to show appreciation.

Before we get into the series I want you to ask yourself this – why is gratitude important?

I believe that gratitude is essential for us to succeed in life. This is not to say that we should never want more or strive for greatness. But having gratitude for the things and people we have in our lives is the best start to any journey.

When times were hard, when I couldn't see a way out, my mum would always remind me of all that we had. From a roof over our heads, clothes on our backs, hot water, food in the cupboard, and that her and my siblings were by my side.

Sure, there was still so much that I wanted, but this grounded me, and helped me look at my life through a lens of gratitude rather than through a lens of disappointment and unmet expectations.

So, what are you grateful for today?

Before you embark on this journey, I encourage you to take a few minutes to make a list of all the things you are grateful for.

Observe how you change your posture, your attitude and your demeanour when you think of these things.

I believe that no matter how tough things get, there is ALWAYS that one ray of light, despite all the challenges that helps you realize that the best is yet to come.

In our life, let's trust that we will see more sunshine than rain, but when it does inevitably pour be prepared with our umbrella so we don't get caught out in the showers.

So let's be grateful for what we do have and be expectant for all that will come our way.

Series 1: My Life Has Purpose

You are uniquely and wonderfully made. Priceless because there is no one like you in this world. Who you are and how you experience the world is unique to only you. Your talents, skills and passions are also unique.

You are YOU for a reason. You are in this world for a reason and for a purpose. There is so much beauty and wonder inside of you with your own unique blueprint. There is PURPOSE within you, so let's get it out!

Definition:

Purpose: Purpose-built, a sense of resolve or determination.

Your life's purpose will not only transform you but the lives of others around you.

Knowing your purpose and using it to its fullest potential is a magnificent gift.

Your purpose is your determination for the things you want to achieve. It is where your aims, goals, visions, and passions come to life.

"The purpose of life is not to be happy. It is to be useful, to be honorable, to be compassionate, to have it make some difference that you have lived and lived well."

* Ralph Waldo Emerson*

Motivational Activity:

Define yourself:

- Who are you?
- What do you stand for?
- What are you priorities?
- Why do you want to achieve them?

Notes:

Motivational Story

In me early teens, I read the life story of Martin Luther King Jr. It stirred my heart in more ways than I could have ever imagined. I remember crying as I read of his shooting and off his passing. I cried because this was a man with a big heart, a beautiful dream and a purpose in life to assist others by bringing light where there was darkness.

To this day, his legacy continues to fulfill this very purpose. He knew his purpose and what he needed to do for others. He brought hope to millions around the world of which I benefited from. Following a purpose, in this example changed a nation. If he had sat on the idea, where would we be today?

Regardless of the hardships and risk he faced daily, he kept true to his purpose and the dreams he had for his life.

I learned early in life that I had to use his example as well as those set by the people closest to me, including my Mother and Grandmother to find and follow my purpose.

I love connecting and helping people. Working with them to build and appreciate their life, with the aim of watching them achieve endless success in their own stories.

This is what my business, my career and my life is all about, using my voice to be an influence of positive change. But the journey will always have bumps and naysayers!

Others have tried to dim my light, tried to derail me with verbal and physical abuse – telling me I would be nothing in life and I should 'stay in my lane'

I knew that wasn't the truth. So, since being told I couldn't and wouldn't be accepted into college, get that dream job, buy a car or find a partner by my professors, colleagues, friends and family I have committed everyday to never stop pursuing my purpose and helping others reach and find theirs.

It often seems in life like little progress has been made, but when I look back at how far I have come, it fuels my heart to keep going to see what is next.

To me, living a good life means that I never stop striving to help others, as I truly believe that this is my purpose in life. Don't despise small beginnings, and don't be disheartened with small steps – they lead to bigger results.

Your purpose does not always point to career. Yes, it is a primary focus, but my purpose is also supporting my friends, plugging into communities and looking after my immediate family as we face our individual challenges.

I always knew that finding my purpose in life is a gift, as many others do not know or live in their purpose yet.

My purpose was clear from my upbringing, using my story and where I came from to help heal, grow and motivate others.

Sharing my story and letting people know that if I can come from a broken home of abuse, impoverished, childhood sickness in a third world country, dragged halfway around the world to isolation in a place with a different language and denied an education by your own father to then become a Scientist with a Masters degree from Oxford now living in Vancouver walking in my purpose then you can too.

However for some it may take a lot more searching. My vision will always be to help you find your path and equip you to live your life of purpose.

Let me share with you these beautiful words below by MLK that stirred my heart in a time of need and forced me to look deeper within myself and into my purpose and accept me and it.

I want to ask you a question: What is your life's blueprint?

"Whenever a building is constructed, there is usually an architect who draws it up, and that blueprint serves as the pattern to guide the building project. A building is not well erected without a good, solid blueprint.

Now each of you is in the process of building the structure of your lives, and the question is whether you have a proper, solid and sound blueprint.

May I suggest some of the key components that should be integral in your life's blueprint.

Number one in your life's blueprint should be a deep belief in your own dignity and your worth. Don't allow anybody to make you feel like you're nobody. Always KNOW that you count. Always KNOW that you have worth, and always KNOW that your input has an ultimate significance.

Secondly, in your life's blueprint which you must have as a basic principle is the determination to achieve excellence in your various fields of endeavor. You'll be determining as the days, and years unfolds what you will do in life — what your life's work will be. So, set out to do it well.

When you have the blueprint, you will be able to start with the foundations and the structure. Building without an idea and purpose will lead to something that is mis-mashed and disjointed"

"If you can't fly then run if you can't run then walk if you can't walk then crawl, but whatever you do you have to keep moving forward."

Martin Luther King, Jr

Series 2: My Potential is Limitless

Your potential is limitless. Each day that passes by, you nurture your potential by working hard to fulfill your life's purpose, dreams, and goals. With this, you are sowing a seed for yourself and your future. **You are the only thing** that can prevent yourself from not reaching your goals or potential in life.

Definition

Potential: Possible capable of being or becoming.

A potential simply means having the capacity to develop and grow into something incredible in the future. This can include taking care of your health, career, friends, family, self-improvement, and finances. Knowing your potential in life requires a certain amount of self-confidence and self-belief.

Your potential determines what you are capable of being in this life, even if it is still in the developing phase. You already have the potential to achieve incredible and amazing things in your life. It is a daily work in progress, therefore, you must put action into growing and realizing your potential.

Don't just live up to your potential - smash through it and show that you can live a life without limits.

"Potential is a priceless treasure, like gold. All of us have gold hidden within, but we have to dig to get it out."

Joyce Myers

Motivational Activity:

- What characteristics do you believe about yourself?
- What do you see as your ceiling in life?
- What are some of the roadblocks (i.e. Money, Friends, Education) that can hinder you from growing into your potential?
- How can you smash through these roadblocks?
- What can you do today to nurture your potential?

Notes:

Motivational Story

I was fourteen years old, when it became crystal clear to me that the world is filled with so many possibilities and I knew I had to work hard to ensure my potential was not wasted.

I grew up in an environment that had both positive and negative effects. Regardless of how much my mother tried to shield me from our negative environment and upbringing, I realized later on in life that my state of mind and wellbeing was affected negatively.

I sit here writing this as a married woman, but I never thought that would be the case. The main example of marriage we have is our parents. I was told that I was never going to be good enough for someone to love by my father, the same man that continually beat and stole from my Mother and disappeared from our lives at a moments notice only to appear again when the well was dry.

Two issues arose from these situations that affected me for many years. Trust and self-worth. These things can be hard to shake off if we don't push forward and surround ourselves with the right people and the right tools. It can cut off our potential.

I fought so hard to ensure that they wouldn't stick or become a part of me because deep down, I believed and still do now that those negative words and those actions were not my truth or life's truth.

When you grow up listening to someone you love, adore or respect, telling you that your life will be worth nothing, this predisposes you to feel as if you have nothing to offer to them, yourself, and the world in general. It is hard to stand firm and not let doubt creep into your mind that what they say might be true. This was my reality, and it might be yours too.

Monitor your thoughts, lock the false ones away that are suffocating you and costing you from fulfilling your potential.

The thought of traveling came to my mind at a very young age - seeing the world, finding my truth and realizing my potential. I was so excited about the idea of leaving the negative comments behind even if for just a short moment, especially the limitations put on me by my father that had adverse effects on me indirectly.

I packed my bags and embarked on a new adventure. I thought I would be scared being away from my mum and siblings alone for the first time, but I found out that I welcomed the change and the new environment well. I found things I loved, and I met incredible people along my journey that shared their love of traveling, community and sisterhood with me.

The change of scenery really shaped the next few years of my life. Because in that moment I had stepped out, seen a different world, seen how people hustle for what they love, hustle for their passion and see the importance of what being brave can bring.

It wasn't always easy to follow my dreams, but I stayed true to myself and never gave up. I knew that if I did stop, I would be giving power back to negativity. I was determined to not let dream stealers (such as; self-doubt, insecurities, lack of confidence) have the final say.

I knew I was growing up fast and in many ways now, I have grown to become better and stronger because of these experiences. I have the opportunity to keep growing, and my daily progress will continue to lay the foundation of my best self, because I know I can do more and be better. Looking back at the goals I have achieved, it is just amazing.

There is always more I can do for my life and for others, and that continues to drive and push me forward.

Traveling, reading inspirational and motivational books about the lives of others who have gone through a similar path has helped me tremendously to forge a path ahead. Spending time with my mother and my closest friends pushed me to stay true to who I am.

I kept seeing daily changes in my life through the hard work I put in because I never allowed myself to settle for anything less than what I deserved.

I choose a different path for myself, and here I am today still breaking grounds in my personal life, my career, and business and it is only the beginning.

I would not be the woman I am today if I believed all that I was told, saw truth in everything I had seen and put those limitations on my life.

Your victories might not seem much to others, but that is not important as your journey is personal. Don't focus on someone else, rather focus on your remarkable progress and where you are heading.

It may not necessarily be traveling for you, but whatever it is that you can do to step out of the negativity, do it without hesitation and follow your gut.

By changing the tune you are giving yourself time to think, see your potential in a clear and beautiful light.

You have what it takes, you have limitless potential so don't give into fear or stop encouraging and cheering yourself forward.

"The only person you are destined to become is the person you decide to be."

Ralph Waldo Emerson

Series 3: I Am Fearless

Fear is a part of life and in most cases, it cannot be avoided. But know that you are capable of being fearless if you exercise your willpower. It begins the moment you let go of all those reasons in your mind as to why you can't achieve your goals.

Be brave. Don't let fear dominate you, because fear is nothing more than an obstacle that stands in the way of progress.

Definition

Fearless: Being brave, bold, courageous and confident

When you find your truth, own it and it's power to overcome the fear. This is the first step toward overcoming your fear. Although, this will not produce an instant result, but it is something that you can practice, teach and believe in yourself every day, in order to truly overcome the burden of fear.

Beware of **dream stealers** because they come in the form of many shapes and sizes (such as; fear, insecurity, lack of motivation, pride) that make you forget who you are. They also leave you too busy with irrelevant thoughts and emotions, thereby preventing you from chasing your true dreams and costing you your happiness in the process.

Beware of low self-value. Diminished self-value makes you believe the lies others have said to you, which can cause you to believe that you are of little importance. Be aware of such situations that will cause you to lose your confidence and your vision. **Know your triggers**.

Fear is only powerful if we continue to feed into it. Fear is irrational, so even when presented with counteracting facts, it can take over and overwhelm us. Replace fear with **Faith** and believe that everything you want is coming your way.

"Being fearless doesn't mean living a life devoid of fear, but living a life in which our fears don't hold us back."
Arianna Huffington

Motivational Activity:

- What makes you happy?
- What makes you scared?
- What makes you excited?
- If there were no boundaries – what are the things in your life you wouldn't be afraid to share with the world?
- What would you have done differently with your life knowing what you know now?

Notes:

Motivational Story

On the other side of fear is ***Freedom***.

I spent a big part of my life being afraid of letting people see me as sad, lonely, broken, depressed and vulnerable. I was often encouraging my friends to live fearless lives, while I struggled in my own fears.

I was struggling financially, unable to afford an education. While boxed in by fear, negative thoughts started to creep in – that I wouldn't get an education and start an exciting future, that I wouldn't get a good job, that my situation at the time wouldn't change and that I wouldn't get to do what I dreamt of doing. My fearful thought steamrolled and overwhelmed me and made my situation seem impossible when it simply wasn't.

My mind often said, "you may as well quit now," "don't bother," "your life is fine with being okay." But I kept my dream alive by taking on extra work, cutting costs and saving hard, because I could see what the future held and I knew that if I braved it and let go of fear, and when we manage the thoughts in our mind we find our freedom to chase what stirs our heart.

I didn't let my circumstances change where I wanted to go. It's time to remove the attitude of 'this is just the way it is,' you are designed to achieve more and fear is the only thing stopping you. It is never too late to change your narrative.

I relentlessly pursued the goals and desires I had for my life. I found a way to finish college got a job as a Biomedical Scientist and now running my own business. These powerful moments are amongst the achievements that came from finding my freedom and living in my truth.

Instead of living in fear, I chose to live fearlessly and confidently, leaving behind self-doubt, insecurities and all the things that were holding me back from living in my purpose.

We need to remember that life will not always be smooth sailing. Life is not always great, because tomorrow is uncertain. Things happen that we can't prevent and that we would prefer didn't occur in the first place.

But if life was always wonderful, would we appreciate all the amazing things or would we take them for granted? We can learn so much about ourselves when we go through challenges and problems.

I had saved for so long - my dream was to buy a house and I was close to achieving this goal. But out of nowhere, in a situation I thought was sorted struck disaster. The money I saved was needed to support someone I loved. The money I had was not enough and I had to take out an emergency loan for a lot and needed it now!

I didn't hesitate for a second, but after a moment I felt happiness that I had helped a loved one in need, followed by sadness as I felt like I had taken a step back and worried about what was next. These thoughts and feelings were around my neck for a long time and affected my life - the fear was strong.

It is never a comfortable situation when you're in the middle of adversity or challenges, but when you get through it, you can look back and see what you have learned from the situation and be proud of where you are.

The good times will always come when you keep pushing. What was meant to take me six years to pay off, took only one year - a job came in Belgium where I could earn enough in six months to pay it all off.

The best part - before I took out the loan, my plan was to come and live in Canada but I was stopped by this circumstance I thought was terrible. But being forced to stay meant reunited me with my now Husband and as I mentioned earlier...Move to Canada!

Challenges are an opportunity to grow, learn and take you on incredible journeys. Don't let it box you in but learn from them and keep moving forward.

Being able to bounce back and recover from adversity makes us stronger and contributes to our dreams becoming a beautiful reality.

I developed resilience and found my strength from all the adversity I withstood. I learned how to handle difficult situations I was faced with.

By knowing and living in my truth, I became resilient, I found a strong sense of self-belief and faith in my strengths and capabilities. Even though it hasn't always been easy, I made sure I stayed true to myself.

Don't let fear hold you back from chasing your dreams, chasing what sparks your heart and passion.

From adversity comes opportunity and from living fearlessly becomes unlimited possibility.

"A situation will always repeat itself until we learn the lesson we are meant to learn from it."

Efe Fruci

Series 4: I Am Confident

Confidence comes from embracing who you are. To live in our potential often requires us to step out of our comfort zone to try new things. In life, your confidence will grow with your choices.

Choosing to believe in yourself and being confident is key to living in your potential. You must be willing to try and do something you haven't done before, and this is a great tool to help you achieve something you haven't or didn't think you could achieve.

Definition

Confidence: boldness, self-assurance, and poise, full-trust: belief in the reliability or trustworthiness of a person or thing.

Some of us have lived a life where we have followed the opinions or demands of others to appear as a 'nice person.' We never pull back the veil and only let people see what we want them to see. As a result, we may have lost ourselves in our efforts to win their approval or friendship. But is it real?

Living this way allows frustration, depression, sense of rejection, lack of confidence and even resentment to take root in our thoughts and emotions. When you hide who you are you simply cannot grow and walk in your true journey.

Remember that our emotional gates must be flexible enough to allow or prevent entry of influences as we determine, whether they are negative or positive influences.

Don't be afraid to show the world how valuable you are. If you have something in your heart, be brave enough to share them.

Be confident by believing in yourself and your capabilities to make it happen.

Confidence in who you are, confidence in your moral standing and confidence in your dreams will take you a long way to achieving your potential.

"Noble and great. Courageous and determined. Faithful and fearless. That is who you are and who you have always been. And understanding it can change your life because this knowledge carries a confidence that cannot be duplicated any other way."

* Sheri L. Dew*

Motivational Activity:

- What does confidence mean to you?
- Where are you most confident about in your personal and professional life- Make a list?
- What are your confidence 'power poses' (i.e. Superman or Wonderwoman or simply standing tall with your hands in your pockets) Stand up wherever you are and do it now!
- Do you live your life based on the expectations of others?
- Are you confident in your personal and professional life?

Notes:

Motivational Story

What you think of yourself is much more important and valuable than what others think of you. Do not get in the habit of living your life through someone else's expectations to avoid limiting your potential.

When you look in the mirror, are you proud of the person staring back at you?

Ask yourself, how can you expect others to see how incredible you are if you are unable to see it for yourself?

I discovered my own self-confidence when I was sixteen years old. After finding myself in an unimaginable situation, I traveled from Belgium to a Sweden. I left negativity, abuse, rejection and so much hardship behind to see what else was out there in the world, to expand my knowledge, seek new opportunities that might give me a new lease on life.

Returning home a few months later, and feeling rejected by my biological father (again) I was heartbroken, but as time progressed, I forgave him and found peace for my own mental well-being.

I also discovered that it was not my business to understand why he did what he did. Instead I focused my time and energy supporting my mother and my amazing siblings I have been blessed with. I invested my energy into my future into the people and things that really mattered.

My self-confidence grew even bigger the moment I witnessed the birth of my younger sister as my mother's birthing partner. This brave decision brought me so much joy that after all the years of praying for a baby sister, she arrived. I had renewed hope in a hopeless state, and it brought meaning and clarity back into my life.

(On a side note – This moment sparked another career I pursued in Midwifery and today as a Doula!)

I also realized just how determined, brave and fearless I became as I relentlessly stood up and protected my mum against domestic abuse during her pregnancy. To see a new life being born from a toxic situation gave me a new perspective on life.

When I say I discovered self-confidence, it is because while growing up, I did not have confidence in myself, even though I often felt it from doing what I believed was right- standing up and speaking up for myself or those I care for.

I just couldn't tap into my self-confidence or use it to the fullest as I was so unsure what confidence was all about. Yet, I was determined to keep on trying to bring more of it in me.

During the ages of twelve to fifteen, my confidence was at an all-time low, as I truly came to the realization that I had one parent, the man who was supposed to love me unconditionally and protect me at all cost, did not care about my well-being - whether I was alive or healthy. All he ever did as a form of communication was either a slap to my face or via direct verbal abuse.

I struggled from his rejection and disconnection toward me. I wasted a lot of time thinking, feeling and asking myself if there was something wrong with me that would make him act the way he did towards me. Had I done something wrong, was I not pretty enough and why doesn't he care or want me as I am, especially as I watched other parents love and accept their children.

The one thing that got me through this period of my life was having my mother and grandmother constantly reminding me of who I am, especially when I couldn't see it for myself.

They made sure I was aware that even though my father didn't see my worth and value, it wasn't my fault and it doesn't make me any less special. They both showed me through their actions and words that I was loved, cherished and priceless.

Fortunately, I also had my brothers - three great men in my life that showed me what a real man does for the people they loved. They set the very best examples for me.

Confidence is not built alone, it is built up on community with the right people, all striving to lift each other together, rather than at the expense of each other.

The moment I understood the true meaning of forgiveness, self-respect and appreciating my worth and value, I began working towards letting go of all the pain that was destroying my life: I was able to set myself free. I became free mentally, emotionally and personally. I unlocked the strong woman in me that was always there but just needed a good nudging.

For the first time, I chose myself, saw the truth that was spoken into my life and felt the love from all the people that truly mattered to me. I believed in myself and my future more than before, and had others who believed in me, encouraged me and lifted me. This all helped me to start living my life in my truth confidently.

I know it is not always easy to find confidence, but I am telling you now that IT IS INSIDE YOU. You have to continue to nurture it to life. When you are ready to live in your truth to show the incredible person that you are, you won't ever want to look back, especially when you see how far you have come.

Show yourself to the right person, to someone who cares for you and your general wellbeing and you will grow. But hide and only scratch the surface and the past, the feelings of self-doubt and lack of confidence will stay.

I encourage you to find joy in your uniqueness. We are all different, and this is a good and beautiful thing. The way you see people, love others, express your feelings, tolerate pain or even care for people is unique to only **YOU**.

You are awesome the way you are because there is no one in this world who is like you. So take the time you need and keep on building your confidence.

Remind yourself each day that passes by how incredible you are.

Try something new and daring each day that takes you out of your *comfort zone into your confidence zone*. Quit apologizing for being you, for being confident, brave, different, and unique.

Be proud of who you are and who you are becoming. Let your confidence not only shine through you but use it as a tool to empower, inspire and motivate you and others.

"You gain strength, courage, and confidence by every experience in which you really stop to look fear in the face. You are able to say to yourself, 'I lived through this horror. I can take the next thing that comes along."

Eleanor Roosevelt

The idea of living a prosperous life of worth is by placing a value on your life; a value that is not validated based on someone else's ideas but yours. A value that cannot be bought no matter the price tag.

You value something you love, and that is a natural instinct isn't it? So why not love and value yourself too?

Definition

Value: important, meaningful, significant

Worth: Virtue, priceless

Your value has nothing to do with what you think. Your value is not based on where you were born, where you went to school, your relationship status, family circumstances, financial situation or popularity (friendship is quality not quantity)

Your value is not determined by the opinions of others, nor is it determined by our failures.

Your value is connected to you as an individual, because it is who you are. So no matter what people say, names they call you or see you as, you are valuable because you are priceless. You have worth because you are worth loving and important because you are YOU for a reason.

So stay true to yourself and don't let these external circumstances change or distract you from the true you.

Your past and present failures are a part of you, but it shouldn't define you in a negative way. Instead, it should help you grow and learn. All your experiences can act as a springboard in understanding your true value and finding your life's purpose. Your life is valuable and so are you.

Therefore, if you put a small value on your life, you are not fully giving yourself all the worth, care and love you need and deserve.

"Self-Respect, Self-Worth And Self-Love All Start With yourself. Stop Looking Outside Of Yourself For Your Value"

Rob Liano

Motivational Activity:

- What is your self-value determined by?
- If you put a price tag on your life how much are you worth?
- What does your worth and value mean to you?
- Are you spending all your time waiting for valuation from others?
- If yes, why and how can you work towards appreciating your value and worth?

Notes:

Motivational Story

Say to yourself; "I am valuable because I am. I have worth because I am worthy."

Growing up, I thought my value was based on my family status and the houses we had and lived in but it wasn't all about that.

Despite the many phases of my life, I grew up having the best things, because my mother work tirelessly and ensured that we had everything we needed, thus allowing us to learn the true value of hard work.

So when my life took a sad turn, when we lost everything (our house, car, and money), the things I once considered valuable was taken away from us. I realised that I had based a lot of my value and worth on material things.

Starting over and finding a way to survive day by day, it quickly and painfully became clear that I had people in my life that loved me and wanted me around because of the things we had.

My mother was known through her multiple businesses and as a well-respected High School Professor in Nigeria. So when people became aware of my family issues, a lot of these 'friends and extended family' left our lives as quickly as they came in.

I had to learn the hard way. I realized they had placed my value on those physical things rather than valuing me as a person.

Of course, when it sank in that they saw no use in associating themselves with me or any members of my family, some made a loud noise of it, while others silently left our radar.

I thought my worth and value as a young girl and as a person was tied to my family's financial and socioeconomic status. I felt like I was nobody when people started leaving my life like flies.

But one day when I was fed up from feeling sad, angry and disappointed, I asked myself, why does it matter? Why am I feeling like this? Why am I validating all my life's value from this situation?

Instead of showing my family and I support, all we ever received were negative responses from the same people who once called themselves friends and family, and it soon became clear that I didn't really know them as much as I thought I did.

Are these the type of people you want in your life anyway? I would say a big NO!

I saw that regardless of our circumstances and what was happening around me, I was still alive and doing fine and there were still some genuine people in my life. The people that truly cared brought us food, clothes often simply calling or stopping by to chat or to check in on us.

They kept encouraging and reminding me that all the things that I had lost wasn't the end of my life, that I am valuable and worth so much to them with or without those things. That feeling alone made me stronger.

I have value and worth because I have a treasure inside me that always sees the beauty in every situation. I have the strength to raise myself up when I have been kicked down and the capacity to love others when I wasn't loved back.

I have a compassionate heart to share whatever I have with others and I am determined on remaining hopeful that difficult situations do not and will not last forever, rather they teach a valuable lesson about who we truly are.

My Mother is an example of this. She had lost it all, through no fault of her own but remained just as caring, faithful and loving to those around her than ever before. I took this approach and applied it to the way I treat people no matter what their situation. Because of this circumstance I was still me, just a better version.

I tell you now that when you learn how much you're worth, you'll stop giving people discounts to come into your life and mess with your mind to alter your way of thinking.

We live in a society that constantly tells us that once we've made a mistake in our lives we can never amount to anything meaningful. We are told that our bad decisions can devalued and disqualified us from ever reaching certain aspirations.

This makes us struggle with our own self-belief and abilities to achieve our goals. We lose value because of our mistakes and can spiral into our comfort zone, never daring to try again.

Believe in yourself, never underestimate the value of your life. You were made for a reason, and even though some days it may seem hard to see your value, always trust the process.

Stay on the path of your journey, believing that you have enough value to complete your journey and that your moment will come.

It's important to spend some time alone learning about yourself through self-reflection. How do you know how much something is worth if you don't know yourself? Would you buy a car knowing that it has no engine? So don't sell yourself short but get to know what is under the hood.

Being around positive people who see your shining light and are supporting you further into your life can assist you with this. Surround yourself with people who see you for you, see your value, and see your worth.

Then ensure to check yourself once in a while and see if you are still on the right track. You should be able to ask yourself "Who am I doing life with and how do we all lift each other up?"

Embrace the person you are now and the person you see yourself becoming tomorrow. Never let anyone determine your worth or tell you who or what you should be. What you say and who you are matters.

Because I tell you now, there is great power in self-acceptance- that if you accept who, what and where you are each and everyday, in that moment, you will sense a stronger underlying feeling- and that feeling is what I have come to know as HAPPINESS.

It's all about making peace with yourself and the freedom to be.

Always remember, that your value doesn't decrease based on someone's inability to see your worth.
Unknown

Series 6: I Am Enough. I Am Loved

This world is a beautiful place. We as individuals see it differently and that is also a beauty in itself. You matter simply because you exist in this beautiful world. Celebrate you and see that you are enough for YOU.

Definition

Enough: Sufficient, fully (whole)

Loved: A feeling of deep affection towards yourself

You should never become someone else to please others. Who you are and the person you are becoming is something you should be proud of at all times. Remind yourself you are enough, even if you are still figuring out several things in your life. It shouldn't stop you from being enough or loving yourself.

We are constantly changing and learning new things about ourselves and always developing, but the key is and I will say it again is to stay true to yourself.

Loving yourself and knowing that you are enough will open your life to amazing opportunities and friendship. It is then up to you to dive in head first and see what your future has in store.

Say, **I am enough and I am loved**. Often, it is great to hear these words being said by someone else, so why don't you also get used to hearing yourself say it as well. Reaffirming these words back into your life.

Each day you feed your soul with these words, you make yourself whole again.

It is about allowing yourself to discover the happiness that's right there inside you right now waiting to be found- waiting to be accepted- waiting for you to be grounded in your body.

"I am WHOLE. I am ENOUGH because I AM"

Efe Fruci

Motivational Activity:

- What does being enough and being loved mean to you?
- Think of a new way you can show yourself you are enough and loved by you and capture it below.

Notes:

Motivational Story

I Am Enough and I am loved.

I thought I wasn't enough or loved after I went through my first rejection at a young age. Then again, as I started applying for colleges after ten years as a stay at home caregiver. I felt I wasn't qualified enough whenI applied for jobs. I didn't feel I had what it takes and I wasn't exactly what they needed.

After unsuccessful job application and interviews I felt confused. I countlessly asked myself why me? Why did they say yes to that person instead of me? What was wrong with me? Why can't I find the same job as my peers?

When you do get the job, you're faced with a new questions like why is the new person being promoted instead of me, when I have been here putting in the work for much longer than they have?

In reality, I had many negative reasons that would have kept me boxed in by fear if I had allowed it take over my mind and thoughts. Instead, I chose to fight back and to work harder for what I wanted and knew I deserved.

The sooner we can realize that rejection is part of life and it isn't something we should see as a bad thing, then the fear of worrying if we are enough will diminish.

When I walk into an interview or a client meeting, I always give my all. I do my research ahead of time, I get my best clothes ready (look your best to feel your best!) and I imagine every scenario, question and test that might come up.

But if it doesn't go my way in the end, I know I did my best and that a better opportunity is waiting for me. This door is an experience, but was someone else's to walk through.

In times when others couldn't see that I was enough, in my relationships, friendships and in my career, I chose not to feel defeated or unloved. I had to accept that it wasn't or isn't my time yet. I focused on learning more, and doing more to better my chances for the next opportunity that comes around.

There were many moments when I felt humiliated and defeated, when someone who was my junior got promoted before I did and then I had to train them for the same job that I already knew how to do.

I have had more than my fair share of humiliation, setbacks and sad moments that left me feeling like I wasn't good or smart enough. I cried out in pain, released the frustration either by screaming into my pillow so no one will hear me, crying myself to sleep more times than I can count, yet I remained hopeful and grateful in all things believing that the next day will be my day.

I had to remind myself of the journey from being unable to go to college to acquire the degrees I now have, that put me in this amazing position. Without having that degree, my journey to work in the field of my interest would have been much harder and would have taken me even longer to achieve. Sometimes it is good to look back at previous accomplishments when times are hardest to remember what you can achieve in your present.

So if I had been given that promotion, I may not be here fulfilling my goals, visions, and desires today, I encourage you to see that there is more to life, there is more for you, there is something better when a situation doesn't go your way the first or hundredth time.

The strength is in knowing that when one door closes, a better one will fly open at the right time for you.

Rejection is simply a step in our life direction – not backwards but forwards. A rejection just as much as an acceptance is a part of the journey, so do not be disheartened.

Whether you are rejected, accepted, promoted or demoted, these are part of your life GPS helping you to make sure that you are going the right way, growing in the process and moving onward towards the right destination.

Remind yourself every day of every moment that you are enough. You are a masterpiece that should be treasured. Don't rush to build yourself up into someone that you are not, as every masterpiece takes time to become something extraordinary.

Poem- I Am Enough

I am not sorry for being me.

I am not sorry I am confident, bold, resilient, fearless and beautiful.

I am not sorry I chased after a dream you told me I couldn't have.

I am not sorry for being strong and enough to know I have worth.

I am not sorry for being blessed with a purpose and unlimited potential.

I am not sorry for being happy.

I am not sorry for who I AM and for never giving up.

I am not sorry now or ever for reaching for the skies, for dreaming bigger and for expecting the best for my life.

I am not sorry for finding love and choosing happiness.

I am not sorry for fighting so hard for the life I have now.

I am not sorry for wanting and knowing there is more for me.

I am not sorry for being brave enough to share my story to empower, motivate and encourage others.

I am not sorry because I AM ENOUGH FOR ME.

I wrote this poem above to encourage you to stop apologizing for who you are to stop apologizing for chasing your dreams and to stop saying sorry for being you.

Having confidence, having a purpose and chasing a dream can often scare others around us. So before you start this series, understand that you don't have to be sorry for being true to yourself and you certainly shouldn't apologize for reaching for the stars.

People are quick to point out your faults, quick to critique and eager to comment on how you should or shouldn't live your life. But I believe that we should always encourage everyone to be true to themselves, be open about who they are and create an environment where everyone feels free to express themselves.

Will we ever see a world that is positive, open and encouraging to all beliefs, dreams and attitudes? Maybe. But it starts with each individual taking ownership of who they are and embracing it no matter what anyone else says or thinks.

It will not always be an easy ride, but I encourage you to get people around you, who see you, love you and support you for being YOU.

Understand YOU ARE ENOUGH.

Series 7: I Have The Power Of Choice

If you are reading this now then you have the power of choice. You have the free will to make choices and decisions about your life.

You have the power to decide how you want your life to be, the power to choose who you want to love, the house you want to buy, the school you want to go to and the power of choice to love yourself.

Definition

Power of Choice: Having the free will to make the decisions pertaining to your life.

Each day, we make decisions just as little as what to eat for lunch, what to wear to work, which book or books to read for the weekend, can I afford to buy a car. Then, some decision-making are also big, which includes paying bills, applying for the right jobs, buying your first home or who to be in a relationship with.

Some of these decisions may affect the lives of others around you. Some may not be able to see your vision or reasons behind the choices you have made. It doesn't matter if they can't for as long as you know you are making positive and healthy choices that will help ensure you stay on track on your life's journey.

Don't be overruled with other people instructions on how you should live your life, especially if their opinions are coming from a negative place. You always have a choice.

"Use wisely your power of choice"

Og Mandino

Motivational Activity:

- Do you have the power of choice over your life? If not, why and how can you reclaim it?
- What situation in your life is affecting your power of choice?
- What does the power of choice mean to you?
- Do you find decision-making difficult?
- Are you in an environment that is bringing you joy or pain?

  If yes to joy - how can you maintain it?

  If yes to pain- what can you do now to change your situation in order to turn your pain into your power?

- How can you positively change the way you respond when faced with a challenge or adversity?

Notes:

Motivational Story

For so many, the power of choice is stripped away for so many reasons. Making choices may be easy for some, and it may not always be as easy for others because some of your choices will challenge you on who you believe you are to your very core.

I remember the first time my power of choice was stripped away, I was in a new country and was excited for the day to come so I can start college in the fall. Little did I know that was not possible.

When I asked why, I was not only slapped for daring to ask, I was also verbally insulted that it wasn't in the cards for someone like me, and that I was never going to be anything in life, and that I should stop thinking about it forever. My life's plan was being mapped out, but not by me.

When I was fifteen walking to my French class, I watched as a car violently pulled over next to me, a strange man leapt out and grabbed my arm, screaming that I had to come with him now.

Screaming, looking for help, but there was nobody around. Finally, an old lady came out of her house and the man calmed his voice and said ' Your Dad has asked me to come and get you' We had left my Father's grip about a year earlier so this came as a shock. Luckily the women distracted him enough that I was able to loosen his grip and ran away and hid in safety.

A few years after this history repeated itself again as I watched my younger sister who was in my care, at the young age of four be dragged out of my arms and in our home by two armed cops while our mother was at work.

My Mother came rushing to meet us at the courthouse where they took my sister, she found out both my sister and I were both placed in two separate rooms. Little did we know that will be the last time we would see my little sister and take her home for the next nine month.

She was transferred without our consent- without us explaining to her what was happening- without access to her favorite toys or books. After waking up in a happy and safe home that morning, just like that her innocence was taken away from her. Our light was dimmed as we were told she had been placed in an orphanage when she had both parents still alive.

It was the most painful chapter of my life. Yet, I knew I had to stay strong for my mother, my sister and myself. I remember fighting everyday for us to be reunited with her again, and it took almost a year before she was allowed to come back home.

My sister's choice was taken away by someone that did not want her, just out of spite. I felt ashamed that I couldn't protect the one thing I swore to protect in our own home. My Mother had no choice in where my sister was placed and I was left to pick up the pieces of our broken family.

At this point in my life I felt like my choices were limited. With no job, no money and no friends to confide in, I had only one choice: stay and fight, support my Mother, my family and to get my sister back to us where she belonged.

After a few years of custody battle, a violent public altercation outside the agreed visitation center that sent me to the hospital with a broken jaw, my mother and I fought harder in court to not only prove ourselves fit to care for her, but that my sister will be living in a safe home and only then when the truth came to light were we able to bring her home.

Then again, into my early twenties when I was in college, completing my summer program not only was I verbally abused and bullied by a few students as I struggled with my lessons in class, I also had one of my teachers doing the same thing.

I remember being so excited as I made my way to her office to inform her that I had received feedback from one of the Universities I applied to, and I'm being asked to come for an interview.

I respected her and felt it would be fitting to have her as one of my references. What should have been a thirty minutes conversation of positive advice and interview prepping turned into a sad reality when I heard her say "someone like you and with your background will not be accepted into a prestigious school like that."

Hurtfully enough, it didn't stop there as she went on to say that I am not the ideal candidate they would be looking for. I left feeling so shattered and helpless, like I was physically beaten and wishing the floors would just open and suck me up in it.

Yet, as I stood up from the chair, I said back to her as I held back tears that "this is your opinion of me, I will go off to University and I will be somebody in life." I believed it then and I still believe it now.

Don't get me wrong, I wanted to respond back with something equally as painful, but I held back after I took a moment to think to myself, *what good will it do?*

I want you to remember that you have the power of choice to react or respond either negatively or positively when you find yourself in an unfamiliar situation.

These scenarios for me in a way may be common or similar to others, that feeling of hopelessness and helplessness as if your voice may never be heard, and feeling trapped in your situation or by negative people.

For many others, their power of choice may have been stripped due to even more difficult and unimaginable situations. But my advice to you is that you should never give up hope. Even if you don't always feel it, help is on its way and someway and somehow, it is coming to you.

It is more important that you train your mind to manage your feelings and emotions well in these situations, because how you think when you are in a tough situation can influence your reactions.

Learn to encourage yourself to think positively even in your darkest moments or when faced with a challenging situation. No matter what situation you find yourself in, nobody can ever take away the power of you dreaming of where you want to be.

Watching yourself and recognizing how your mind, feelings, and emotions reacts in a negative and positive situation will become increasingly useful when you need to control your mindset.

I know we see and feel things differently and we humans handle challenging situations in our own way. Try to stop and think before you respond even if it takes a lot from you to think about a positive response. Step back and use that power of choice wisely before reacting.

You will feel much better later when you see that you did not reply to negativity with negativity, but instead you took control of the situation and fought back negativity with positivity.

Start by teaching your mind to address the situation in a healthy and collective manner, so as not to influence your decision-making in a negative way.

Know your triggers and understand what makes you tick. Knowing your trigger ensures you are not forced to become someone you are not or forced to react to a situation that could cost you your integrity.

You may not always be able to change your circumstances or bad things from happening, but you can always take control of your life and future, so that the words you say out of anger do not destroy all the hard work you have done or are doing in your life.

I want to challenge you if you are always quick to respond in tough situations, take time to explore your feelings and the reasons why you do so.

I encourage you to know yourself so you can rise above when you feel you are being attacked negatively, so you can heal, grow and manage your feelings and emotions well when negative words are said to you.

When you learn more about yourself, you'll begin to see changes in your life, in your situation and you will be able to move forward and leave the negativity behind you. Knowledge is power and you have the choice to use it.

"I am not what happened to me, I am what I choose to become!"

Carl Jung

Series 8: I Have A Future

Did you wake up this morning feeling extremely happy, energetic and ready to start the day? Or did you wake up feeling weak, unsure or not ready to face the world?

These are common feelings for so many people. It is not something that should scare you or make you look at yourself differently. If you are feeling one of these ways, it is to show you that you have your 'on and off' days. When you are having your off days, that is when you should work even harder to maintain a positive thinking and mindset.

Definition

Future: *A time regarded as still to come.*

You shouldn't give into the negative thoughts, instead start by believing the truth about yourself by saying "I know I am not feeling great, but I am smart, capable and determined to change my situation and how I am feeling in a positive way."

Believing the truth about yourself is very important, as it will help you see yourself and think in a positive way. You have a future, regardless of what negative words others have said about you or to you directly. You have a future because you deserve it and should be responsible for where it leads you to.

We all have a future whether we see it or not. No matter what we have done in the past, each day is a clean slate.

You have so much to offer the world and yourself, use your dreams and your passions to change not only your life but the life of others around you.

Start each day right, even though some days may be harder by saying '**I am hopeful because I know I have a bright and exciting future'**

Learn to welcome yourself first thing when you wake up in the morning, because happiness I tell you, happens when you welcome each and everyday into your life. Welcome yourself into life and you will find happiness, accept happiness and be happy.

"Yesterday's the past, tomorrow's the future, but today is a gift. That's why it's called the present."

Bil Keane

Motivational Activity:

- What routine do you have in the morning to help you get your day started right?
- What are you passionate about in your future?
- What do you envision for your future?
- What steps can you take to better yourself and your future?
- What negative lies have been said about your life, that you can silence with your truth?

Notes:

Motivational Story

Say to yourself. I have a ***future*** and I will continue to do my best and work hard for it to be everything I deserve.

After years of being verbally abused, always hearing that I would never amount to anything good in life, or that I won't go far in this world, that I wasn't good enough from other people made me struggle. I tried not to believe it could be true, because I knew deep down that I had a future. I knew this wasn't the reason I was created for, to experience pain, betrayal, sickness, and loss.

I never thought that after the age of seven that I will have a future, let alone live to see thirty years old. All I could see at that time throughout my childhood illness was how sick I was and how the doctors told us that it would be a miracle if I survived to see my tenth birthday.

It was hard believing I had a future in those days when all I could see were all the supporting medical devices and tubes going into my arms helping me feed, breathe, grow and stay alive.

Yet even then, my mother believed and knew that there was more in life for me. She told me everyday to fight for the beautiful dreams I was having about my future and she would always say *"Don't listen to your darkest thoughts when you can't see any progress, remember to cherish the moments and hours in the day you get to wake up and fight to do more out of your life and your situation."*

So every year I celebrated a new age and birthday, I knew it wasn't to be taken for granted and even when I made it to thirty years old after hearing doctors say it may not happen for years, I still remained grateful for each day and each moment.

I knew I had a future, a very bright, beautiful, and gifted future then and now and so do you.

I had made it to a place where people told me I wouldn't get to. I had made it to see so much come out of my life regardless of all the bad and unimaginable situations I went through along the way. I have achieved the unachievable for myself and there was so much good to make it all worthwhile.

I saw my future each year in a new light, I accepted my truth and worked hard and I am still working hard to never return to that frail, broken or sick child that I once was. Or returned to the hardship I was surrounded with.

My future is clear to me, for it is designed to be glorious because of the past that I have had and I do know that the present will bring forth my growth and the future will offer me the best that is still yet to come.

Choosing to make your experiences in life count, by looking for the good in all things and living a life true to your values and convictions shows incredible strength and perseverance.

Your future is bright and although you may not feel or know how it will turn out to be, when you do the work required to build yourself daily, the way you think, feel and see yourself, is contributing toward your future.

The way you think today has an impact on your life tomorrow. Tomorrow is a blank canvas, so don't use the dark colours today to ruin the masterpiece.

Don't compare others progress to yours, your future is different to someone else's because your life experiences, decisions and skill set will shape your future- yet, having an attitude of gratitude, you will also shape your future using positive words of affirmation and believing that the best is on the way.

Be patient with yourself because all the work you are putting in your life right now, whether you have help or you are slowly working on it alone will mount up into something extraordinary when the timing is right.

So do not lose sight of how long it is taking you to see a difference, do not lose sight of the *'now moments'* that is building you and getting you ready for your future. Make sure you embrace every situation and challenges life will throw your way.

Focus on how you can be better than the person that you were yesterday. Don't let your past paint the picture of your tomorrow.

Don't let anyone put limitations on your life.

I will say this over and over again, it is important to recognize and think positively about yourself. It doesn't matter if everyone cannot see your potential or purpose in life. Do not give light to negativity.

It doesn't matter if you are unable to find your passion in life or know what you are meant to be doing like others do. Do not allow your mind to go into a dark place filled with lies, insecurities and self-doubt as it will only take you further away from reaching where you want to be.

Remember, everyone is different, everyone dreams differently and everyone sees things differently.

"I have a future, a bright, worthy, unbelievable and extraordinary future that may at times requires hard work. I won't give up hope or give into negative thoughts because I have the determination and drive to try each day I am alive and of good health and of a sound mind to make all my dreams, passions and desires come to life. I won't give up on me"

Efe Fruci

Series 9: I Know My Identity

Knowing and owning your identity is an important aspect of your life as a person. You may know your identity or you may have struggled to know your true self, but either way, it does not decrease your value or worth as a person. Remember that you are incredible and you are not going to accept society, social media or others ideas of what they think you should be like as your identity.

Definition

Identity: The condition of being oneself

Your identity can be influenced by many factors such as social media, people's opinions of you or listening to your own mind which in turn may allow you to see yourself differently or lose your identity completely. It is good to spend time alone with yourself, asking yourself questions that may have popped into your mind occasionally and to really get to know yourself on a mental level.

Often people can be scared to spend time alone with themselves, but how can you truly find yourself and your life's purpose if you never got to know who you are.

The thing is, your identity is based on who you are as a person because of the beautiful way your mind is programmed. You need to know who you are in order to help you see your purpose, this is a path that is guided just for you.

The more you follow this path of your life's journey, the more you see your purpose, your future, the meaning of your life, being able to shape yourself and your life into the way you want it to be and live the life you deserve.

"To know yourself is the beginning of all wisdom"
Aristotle

Motivational Activity:

- On a scale of 1–10 how well do you know yourself?
- Identify and list your three best traits.
- Do you validate your identity from the things of this world?
- Remind yourself (and write it down) of all your best qualities and put it up in your room, office or favorite space so you can see it daily.
- Where do you believe your identity comes from?

Notes:

Motivational Story

The arrangement of a human being is so incredible for a reason, just as your DNA and life's fingerprint is unique only to you, meaning that no one else shares the same DNA as you. Not only is that incredible, but that is what also makes you a unique being.

When I first started to learn and understand science and how the human body works, I was blown away just thinking about all the cells and DNA that we are made up of and I wanted to know more about who I am. It all started with the itch to know why a baby comes out of the womb with white coating called 'vernix caseosa" all over their beautiful body after I witnessed the birth of my younger sister.

I was captivated by curiosity about what makes us human, I was curious to find out what she had that I didn't have, or what I have that she didn't, and what will she be like when she gets to my age and so much more.

I struggled with my identity, especially after years of being bullied, discriminated because of my skin color and physical appearance. I struggled with rejection, feelings of uncertainty of who I was because I gave more meaning to other people's words instead of my own. I saw myself through their eyes instead of through mine. I was losing my own identity without realizing.

I was afraid of owning my story, telling my truth because of what I felt it could do to my family and I.

I refused to communicate or accept who I was, I fought myself at every turn until it started affecting my health, the same health I had once fought so hard to maintain.

As I matured, it became clear to me shortly after my twenty-fifth birthday, that I needed to commit to the change I wanted to see in myself, after my break down which lead me to cut off significant amounts of my hair.

I am not saying cutting my hair was all it took to see myself, but after I came back home, I gazed at myself in front of my mirror for what felt like forever. Immediately, something began to happen, to shift inside me, inside my mind, soul and body as I found myself on the floor in a pool of my own tears.

At first, I was just looking at my new hair which was actually what I wanted, then I saw myself to my very core. I realized I was not seeing myself as a young woman who was lost, broken, rejected, all over the place at times with the messy life and as someone who was so unsure of herself.

I wasn't seeing myself as that anymore because in that moment, right in front of that mirror, I came undone, the chains fear had over me, came undone. Something sparked inside me that refreshed me with a great sense of hope, that made me feel so alive.

It was as if I were seeing myself for the very first time. I saw all my pain that I was hiding from others. I saw the fear that had been holding me back from chasing my dreams. I saw the words of others that I had allowed to hold me back from moving forward, from forging my identity. I also saw the woman I was then and the woman I was maturing to be. She was looking back at me in the mirror.

I was accepting myself as I am, I was loving myself as I deserve to be. I was taking control over my life and my future in a new and positive way, and was no longer influenced by people's preconceived ideas of who I am or who they would like me to be.

Since then, I have never looked back or let go of the incredible and strong woman that was staring back at me in that mirror to ever disappear again.

Who do you see looking back at you when you look into the mirror?

That is not to say that I haven't had my battles along the way. I did go through my bad times, but as my insecurities and self-doubt crept up, I rose up higher, and fought everyday to remind myself of my identity.

When you learn more about your identity it can be scary. This is not easy but is so worthwhile to take the time to do so. Before I knew myself, I felt burdened and a huge weight on my shoulders because challenges would come and overwhelm me. But really knowing yourself builds a strong foundation for your future. Learning not what you are able to handle, but simply how you are going to handle it.

The relationship with yourself is the most important relationship in your life. If you just think for a moment; if you do not have a full understanding of who you truly are, then how are others supposed to know you? You just have to get to know yourself as you would with a new friend, or as you would of someone you are dating.

If you don't know who you are, you might end up seeking validation from other influences and people in your life. You might end up accepting a reality meant for someone else. You might end up not living the life that was made for you.

Your mind is a powerful tool, I call it the engine of my body, it can be shaped in a way that it begins to act and live out what it receives. Therefore, do not be easily changed by the things of this world as it may lead you into more confusion, self-doubt or to even lose sight of your true identity.

Instead teach and nurture your mind to recognize your potential, who you are as a person, who you are becoming and work positively on maintaining your self-identity in ways that bring you hope, meaning, self-acceptance, understanding, and abundant joy.

"Do not conform to the pattern of this world, but be transformed by the renewing of your mind."

Apostle Paul

Series 10: I Can. I Will

What have you never tried in life, but have always been so quick to say you can't do? Yet, when you see other people doing those same things or just being so fearless and bold, you catch yourself saying "Oh I wish I can do that too, or why isn't it so easy for me to be like them?"

Definition:

Can: To be able to have the ability, power or skills.

Will: Expressing future events, expressing facts, abilities, and capacity.

You are able to do whatever you set your mind to do. Whatever you are passionate about, find the reasons behind that passion, the meaning of that thing and also what you hope it will do for you and others around you.

Why don't you do one or more things on your 'I can't do list,' and begin to say "I can and I will." You will be surprised to discover that you are good at a lot of things.

Don't settle for what you know, or look at the box you have been put in and think this is all life can present to you. There are no restrictions being placed on you other than the ones that you are placing on yourself.

I was born in Nigeria, ended up in Brussels, found myself in Texas, California, Chicago chasing after my dream and discovering my heritage then back to Brussels.

I schooled in Oxford and finally back to Brussels. By the time I started this self-motivation book for you, I was back in Oxford, I had left a job that brought no joy, registered and founded my business.

Said yes to marrying my best friend, moved back to Belgium to work in a place that was on my dream list and now building a new life for me and my family in our new home in Vancouver, Canada.

You see, a seed of dream sowed at the age of seventeen was realized in my thirties when I ended up doing the one big thing on my to-do list as an opportunity brought me back to live in Brussels for five month, giving me a new opportunity to change the narrative from what I knew before.

I was able to go back and face my hurtful past and struggles, in turn, help me accept my strength and how I can turn all my past pain into my power.

I was able to find out what it is like to be that woman that gets to work in one of the world's best pharmaceutical industries in Belgium, speaking in French and instead of feeling helpless and of no use, my confidence and self-esteem elevated and I released the negative self-concept that was associated with that past me in both my professional and personal life.

I truly believed that I could and I would, and guess what? I actually did. I spoke and manifested what I wanted into existence through hard work, creating a gallery using my favorite Post-It notes (see below) filled with positive affirmation, a huge can do attitude and I believe you can too.

Here is a small shot of my post-it note motivational wall!

In life, there are some people who are great at some things more than others. What this means is that you have something that you are better at doing that other people may find difficult.

We all have our own strengths and weaknesses. It is all about stepping out in confidence, belief in yourselves and never giving up until you find it.

Having a can-do attitude motivates you to boldly take on new challenges.

Efe Fruci

Motivational Activity:

- Make a list of your skills.
- What is on your can't do list, how can you change it to your CAN do list?
- What haven't you tried, but always wish you had the courage to do?
- What are the things that discourage you from doing or being positive about having a can-do attitude?
- Write one thing you're afraid of failing at and why?
- Write yourself a letter today of how you feel in this moment and read it one year from now to see what you have changed, improved and released since then.

Notes:

Motivational Story

Whatever it is that people have said to you, or you have perhaps said to yourself on many occasions that you can't do (for example; not being creative, not smart enough to apply for that science, tech or office job or start your own business, etc.) without seeing it through, break that cycle by making a list of reasons why *you can* and how *you will.* Now, start ticking off those things off your can't do list for good.

My entire life I have heard things like "you can't, you shouldn't, why would you even?" Yet, at the same time, I was also being reminded by some amazing people why I can, why I should be the amazing woman I will become someday.

I knew it would take me time to see that truth and I am grateful I did. I got myself there with hard work, sticking to the commitment I made to myself to do some good with my life and help others see there is hope through my life's journey and through other positive means like through my workshops, speaking events, supporting other organizations and so much more.

I told myself that I can when people said I could not and would not make it to college or achieve anything in the science world. I worked hard, learnt what I needed to know and then made it through.

I had graduated multiple times, worked across multiple scientific jobs, while registering and running my business. I have met so many awesome people in the process. Simply because I stepped out in confidence saying I can and I will.

I have always been a goal-setter, a big dreamer even though sometimes it scares me and others have crushed it before it could come to life.

Yet, I kept on dreaming, working hard, believing in myself that I can and no matter how long it takes me to get there, I will conquer because I am a warrior, a survivor and knowing it would be a shame if I gave up just when it is about to get even better.

I am a living proof that you can do anything you set your heart to achieve. You can be the person you see yourself becoming if you don't give up working on yourself.

Despite the odds and all that I was faced with and lived through, I have come to believe we can make something beautiful and unapologetically awesome with our lives.

All of this was achieved because I was too strong, too stubborn and so driven to take no for an answer when it came to my life.

If you feel discouraged or demotivated, take a very good look at the list you have made and of all the things you are good at to motivate you. When you discover that you are not so good at it or fail at your first attempt, do not be discouraged or give up easily.

Instead, find out why it didn't work out the first time, seek honest feedback from the people you trust. Take a break to catch your breath and organize your thoughts and start all over again. Most importantly, ask yourself, am I doing this because I want and need to for my personal growth or am I forcing myself to do this because I am comparing myself to others?

Surround yourself with people who challenge you, are not threatened by you and your aspirations but always encourage you on and help you discover new ways to achieve your goals. There is enough room for everyone to succeed and make their way to the top. Find the people that are willing to go there with you.

Tell yourself each day that passes by that you can do whatever it is you are passionate about, whether it is public speaking, writing, working in a lab or driving a train or doing something completely new like joining a sports team, eating alone in your favorite restaurant or singing in a crowd of people. Whatever it is, be sure to *Remind yourself that you are capable*.

It does not matter if you see progress straight away or if it takes days, weeks or years from now.

What is important is *training your own mindset to look for the positives.* Remember when others see trash someone else might see opportunity. When I look back at my life, I don't want to think about the missed opportunities, the lost moments - I want to step right into them even if others or my fear is telling me otherwise.

Train your mind to see yourself with no limits, see your ability to learn new things, take on new challenges and step out when it seems scary. Make a commitment and stay loyal to what you set out to achieve that nothing and *I repeat nothing* will make you betray it.

I can't swim well, yet I found myself bodyboarding in a choppy cold sea in Cornwall in the UK.

Was I scared? Yes. Did I think about drowning? Multiple times. Was my mind open to the possibility of a shark attack? Heck Yes. But as I observed young kids happily boarding in the sea and being so brave, it motivated me to be brave just like they were.

Could I swim up to my knees? Yes

Are there sharks in Cornwall? Not really!

Would I really drown? Maybe, but then there are hundreds of people around me and around ten lifeguards.

At that moment my fear had taken over even though the proof that I would be fine was right in front of me.

So when you stare at a challenge, a change or adversity in the face, train your mind to block the irrational fear and focus on your end purpose and take total control of whatever life throws at you.

We may be approaching the end of this journey, but rest assured that this is just the beginning for you and me.

If you want something, you need to take control of it.
Efe Fruci

YOU DID IT!

Congratulations on taking that first step with "Faith over fear."

Each day, you should feel proud of what you have accomplished. Proud of yourself for taking control of your future.

It doesn't matter how long it took you to get through this book, what matters most is that you used it to equip yourself, your way of thinking and how you see yourself moving forward. Use this as your springboard.

You are encouraged to come back to your book on days where you are in need of a motivational dose of positivity and encouragement to see the progress you have made, the hard work you have put into your book and use that knowledge to keep moving forward.

It is yours to keep as a reminder for as long as you need it. So, you can use it as a reference for your personal-growth, personal-development and keep building your confidence.

There is also an added bonus of motivational exercises that are there to help you dig deeper, to think more positively and more productively.

These exercises throughout the book are there to help you to see how you take and apply what you have learned and gained into your everyday life and even extend the knowledge, wisdom, and understanding to someone else who you know can also benefit from what you have learned.

It has been a pleasure to be on this journey with you and I can only hope that this helps propel you into a world of endless possibilities, a life of limitless abundance and a happy smile when you look at yourself in the mirror.

You are so special, so step out in confidence and show yourself and the world just how awesome you are.

I am and will always be rooting for you as your sister-friend and motivational companion

Motivational Exercises

Do you keep that vision board of your progress in front of you?

This section is additional motivational exercises to help you take all you have learned from this book and start applying them to your everyday life.

These are useful steps that you can also use to set and achieve your desired life's goals in a timeframe that works best for you.

Failure is part of life. I have failed so many times in life and in my business and no doubt I will again in the future, but this should never make us stop trying.

Do not let your failure cost you your voice or your dream. Learn from it and make sure you don't make it repetitive as you move forward.

1. Create a timeline to achieve your goals (Personalizing your Wheel of life).
2. Create your life gallery.
3. Complete your key learning reflection tool.
4. Stick these exercises somewhere you can see and refer to them daily.
5. Mirror exercise

Wheel of life (How to begin)

This is like a life audit. First, think and create a list of all the things in your life that you consider to be your **priorities** (for example, money, career, relationships, education, finance, health etcetera)

(Small Circle - For example, Career)

Set **goals** for each of them (if you find similarities that is fine too)

(Medium Circle- For example: Learn how to start my own business)

Choose the **action plans:** that will help you achieve your desired goals.

(Large Circle- For example: Join a business community group or take business classes)

The aim here is for you to use this circle as a guide to create your own wheel of life. You can add up to eight priorities per wheel. When you know all the priorities, work on them one by one, starting with the most important.

If you need a companion to create your wheel of life, please get in touch. I would love to work with you through your journey. I did this and it was a game changer for my personal and business growth .

This is an example but draw your own and start completing your life audit for your Wheel of Life.

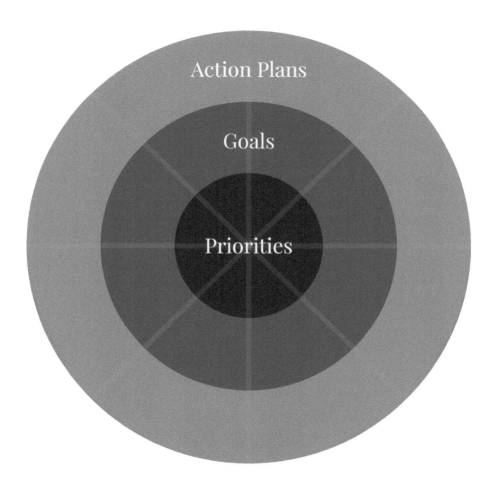

Create your life gallery

I often see my life as an art gallery. So why don't you take a moment and imagine creating a gallery that is filled with love, fun memories, your happiest moments, humor, and beauty, friendships and your perfect dream job? Then, imagine how would you want your life to be? How would you want it to feel or look like?

The purpose is about bringing to life all the beautiful things, people, passion, feelings, relationships and adventures that brings light, happiness and that inspires you. I would imagine you won't want to choose or buy any piece of art that doesn't inspire you or make you feel good about yourself when you look at it. Then think, would you want your life to be like that?

Some of the pieces of your life gallery might bring you sadness, pain and reminders of your struggles. Yet, it will be great to see your life in motion, as they will make you stronger and into the person you are meant to be.

Never forget that what your story creates as your life gallery is a part of you and your journey. It teaches you so much to the point where you can in time embrace, appreciate and be grateful for it all. You should be and feel proud of yourself, feel confident and empowered to hang every piece of your life in your gallery.

Your life gallery should not be something that will keep you stuck in your limitations or in the past, but something that motivates and propels you to move forward. Yet, not invalidating or defining you either as it is a part of a wider tapestry of your life and journey.

You want your gallery to exude fulfillment, peace, honesty, confidence, life without limits or regrets, romance, happiness, excitement, self-acceptance, freedom, fun, creativity, love and abundant joy.

You want it to breathe life into the person you are becoming, your true and authentic self. You want it to speak to you at your core, who you uniquely are in body, mind, and soul. It should breathe comfort, safety, stability, and security without the need of looking to things or others to create or give that to you.

You want your life gallery to breathe your personality, your passion, dreams and desires, eccentricities, love, your talent and skills. It should feature your adventurous side as well as your sense of humor. So think with every part of you, why not take a moment and think about your life gallery using these tips and ideas below.

1. What people, colors, memorabilia, images and places do you see in your gallery?
2. What do you see in your present moment and future to come?
3. Are there masterpieces on the walls of your life gallery and is it filled with unfinished pictures waiting to be completed?

4. What quotations would you like to see in your frames that best reflects you?

Hopefully, when you have truly given all that a thought, and whatever else that you positively want to add to your gallery, I encourage you to keep those pictures and images in your sight of vision. Keep painting even as you go through many changes and keep on loving the masterpiece that is your life.

Check back every now and again on your gallery, add new items to it as you grow, as you cultivate new ways of living your life to the fullest, as you create that place where you can see how far you have come and how far you are willing to go to live a purposeful life.

If we talk about it in fitness terms, see it as a progress picture. When you look at your gallery, you can see how far you have come and that can motivate you to understand how far you can still go.

Key learning reflection tools

What did I learn?

What surprised me?

What did you discover about yourself from reading this book?

Mirror Exercise

When I first did this exercise as mentioned in series 9, I was twenty five years old. I barely knew what it was, how much impact it would later have on my life and how one day it would be called the Mirror Exercise! Since that day, I made an agreement with myself to keep this up.

Everyday I make an effort to practice my mirror exercises before I start and end my day.

At the beginning of my day I repeat and remind myself of my self-declaration to motivate the fearless woman staring back at me. What I feel is a boost of confidence that gives me that extra nudge of courage I deserves to help me kick start the day ahead and tackle any challenges presented.

While at the end of the day, I say my self-declaration out loud and have a self-reflection of my day, how it went and ending it by saying three things I am proud of myself for.

I encourage you to make an agreement with yourself to do these exercises at the start and end of your day. Standing tall and proud by repeating and reminding yourself of just how awesome you are.

If your compassion does not include yourself, it is incomplete."

Jack Kornfield

Bonus 30-minute music meditation

Music is a universal language. Sound vibrates in the air through the songs of birds, trees and in our voices. Using music to build happiness is so much easier than you think. The rhythm, lyrics, beats and vocals all move through our mind and body luring a beautiful musical experience.

Music has been my number one go to when I stressed during exam period, when I felt rejected during job searches, when I experienced lost after my grandmother's passing and even when I want to feel and express joy.

Music can make you emotional, it can help express that which we are unable to say with words to ourselves or to each other and it can mark a happy time in our lives. Music lightens the mood, fills and replenishes our hearts and the smooth effortlessness of being.

Sit or lie down in a comfortable position-whichever you are comfortable with. Turn on your favorite song(s) and turn up the volume. Close your eyes. Relax your body as the rhythm flows through you. Breathe in all that is good and joyful and breathe out all that is unpleasant.

Imagine all your happy moments surrounding you in a glow of light, joy, warmth, peace, and happiness. Open your arms, capture all your goodness by bringing and placing your palms to your heart allowing it to fill you up in loving-kindness, hope and renewed strength.

"May you be safe, be at ease, be joyful. May you be healthy and strong knowing that every life you touch matters– for them and for you. As you shower others with love and kindness, may it always be within your reach.

May you grow healthy communities, friendships and relationships seeing how valuable you are in this world. May you always be connected, committed, intentional and kind to yourself."

Efe is a motivational speaker & women's coach, a writer and workshop facilitator. She is an inspirational leader and founder of Fearless and Empowered.

She inspires, educates and motivates women by helping them learn how to turn their pain into power, their struggles into strengths and how to step up and achieve the unachievable. Whether in our career, our health, our community or our relationships, Efe provides and fuels your soul with tangible and life-changing advice for leading a happier and more successful life.

Efe is a resilient woman who overcame a life-threatening illness that kept her hospitalized for more than six years of her childhood. With Doctors saying she may not live to see her tenth birthday. Efe fought hard for the successful life she is now living.

She turned her pain from physical, emotional and sexual abuse into her power by supporting other victims through focused workshops, speaking engagements and her motivational self-help materials. Helping women speak up, find hope and happiness again, so they can live boldly and reclaim their freedom.

After years of being impoverished and denied an education, Efe's self-motivation and hard work, working three jobs gave her the opportunity to achieve her Higher Educational Diploma in Nursing/Midwifery, a BSc Honors in Biomedical Science and a Masters in Health Science researching postpartum depression and the cognitive effects it has on children.

Not only has she developed a strong and long-lasting relationship with self-confidence, but she also maintained it throughout all her challenges using it to find her purpose - her light that pushes her forward - guides her path and create opportunities where there was nothing but closed doors.

While running a business full-time, Efe also exercises her scientific degree alongside consulting globally for scientific and pharmaceutical companies- specifically in areas such as Cancer, Vaccines, and Medical Technology. She is also completing her certification in Birth and Postpartum Doula; to be able to globally support women during childbirth and postpartum.

Her life is an example to many that with resilience, determination, focused self-drive and hard work, belief in ourselves, faith in our own strengths and abilities that no one (except YOURSELF) can stop you from becoming the person you were created to be, from becoming the person you dream off and are working hard to be.

Her heart and hope for you is that this book through the short insights into her personal life experiences can and will inspire you to take actions to live boldly and freely knowing that with the right support, faith in yourself, you too can achieve the unachievable, knowing that when it comes to your dreams and your future the only person who can give you the life you truly want and desire is YOU.

"Do not withhold good from those who deserve it when it's in your power to help them"

Proverbs 3:27